The Unlikely Relationship

Michael Stary & Willie Bentley

PAGE PUBLISHING, INC.
Conneaut Lake, PA

First originally published by Page Publishing 2018

ISBN 978-1-64350-036-2 (pbk)
ISBN 978-1-64350-037-9 (digital)

Printed in the United States of America

FOREWORD

I was the behavior management teacher for a special program at Ludlam Elementary that was involved in Willie's young life. Prior to his placement in our program, I remember hearing this young child banging on the window coverings outside the classroom—screaming, hollering, and crying. He quickly became the worst kid in the school at such a young age. I remember trying to comfort him during his moments in distress, reassuring him that he would be okay. Such a young soul feeling lost and misunderstood, unable to express his feelings in a non-violent way. After all, growing up in a neighborhood filled with drug buys, gun violence, dysfunctional families, rampart drug use, domestic violence, physical abuse, and a mother—drug addicted. Nevertheless, she did the best she could under the circumstances. Her love was ever present. He never had to wonder about the love she had for him. It was always understood—she loved her baby boy with all of her heart.

A memory I will always treasure is of a conversation with the assistant principal and counselor regarding a phone call from a Dr. Stary, Emergency Department Medical Director of South Miami Hospital. They shared that he was calling the school, inquiring about mentoring a child in reading. Long and short of the matter . . . he was assigned Willie Bentley. We chuckled at the thought.

No one ever assumed that this once-mentoring relationship would last over seventeen years . . . withstanding the chance of time!

Dr. Stary was a welcome relief for this child. He was patient, loving, and non-judgmental. He accepted the challenges of this troubled young child who couldn't read, exhibiting severe emotional/behavioral problems, with open arms, even though their lives were worlds apart. ***White and rich/black and poor***. He became the advocate Willie needed to ensure he received the best educational opportunities afforded him. He provided Willie with opportunities to see the world from another perspective while realizing and respecting where he lived and navigated life. He knew Willie had to be able to go back and survive in his troubled environment.

After forty years as an educator, being employed in various positions, working with exceptional needs children with the most severe emotional/behavioral problems, I've learned that all human beings, regardless of race, gender, color, or sexual orientation, have the fundamental need for positive, loving relationships. We all want to be loved and cared for by someone who thinks we are special. Someone to reassure us that we are good enough. Someone to say, "I'm proud of you." This was especially true with Willie.

Mike and Mom were Willie's greatest cheerleaders. They loved him in different ways, but ultimately the goal was the same. You see, Willie's mom was not perfect, but through her trials and tribulations, he still was able to feel the love she had in her heart for him. A love that *he* continues to crave. He became lost without her. He looked beyond her many issues and saw her heart—her unconditional love.

He continues to look beyond Mike's color and money to see his heart, his genuine love. A love that he has kept sacred even when his friends teased him about "white Mike." Rich Mike. Yes, Mike is able to afford more than most, and Willie's family couldn't, but it was never exploited or taken for granted. It was understood that Willie had to *earn* special gifts from Mike—he had to put forth his maximum effort and always do his best.

This relationship has had its challenges, but through it all is the seam of authenticity and a divine purpose. It has been the undying centerpiece of their lives that remains consistent today. The experiences shared by these two unparalleled lives shows the journey in its fullness. The destination hasn't been reached, the goal hasn't been accomplished, but the unwavering drive is ever present.

The ***Black Lives Matter*** movement has brought to the forefront what it feels like to be racially profiled in society today. It's unfortunate to say that in this relationship both lives have had to endure this unsettling reality of such injustice.

Willie continues to struggle for some purpose and peace in his life. He hasn't received his high school diploma as yet but assures us he's in the process. He's still trying to make sense of a world without his Mom, unfaithful friends, family issues, and no place to truly call home. He and his sisters are looking forward to the day when they can live together once again. No matter what, Mike has been the one true constant in his life.

This project has been an amazing adventure. It afforded me the opportunity to continue to witness the intertwining worlds of these two . . . separated at times but still yoked in love.

Thank God!

PREFACE TO THE SECOND EDITION

Since the publication of this book in 2018 our world has been forever changed by the Coronavirus Pandemic. Those changes continue to unfold and among them appear to be increased isolation, division, blame, and identification of "others". These are precisely some of the tendencies that we had hoped to be able to reduce, not by elegant writing or profound philosophical arguments, but just by the simple juxtaposition of two human beings. As this second edition is published it is our hope that it will be read in that context.

CHAPTER 1

First Meeting

May, 1999: All I Wanted to Do Was Teach One Child How to Read

I was in my forties, a white male from an upper-middle-class family, and an ER physician who had just taken a new position as the medical director of an ER. This gave me flexibility with my schedule. I had moved to a townhouse, which was located directly across the street from an elementary school. My own mother had taught me to read at a very early age, and it had enriched my life so much that I wanted to do the same for another child. As I pictured it in my mind, it would have been a Hispanic female in about the second grade. Her parents might be undocumented and they spoke only Spanish. I would tutor her over the summer, and she would be reading by the start of school in the fall. There is a saying, "Man makes plans and God chuckles." I guess he had a good one on me. At least I got the second-grade part right.

I made an appointment with the school principal and explained my goal. She was kind enough not to laugh at me. She explained that I would have to undergo a background check, and if everything checked out, I could start in the fall. I filled out all of the required paperwork and left. Over the summer I received clearance, and so before the start of school in the fall, I reappeared in the principal's office. I could tell that she was a little surprised to see me, but she introduced me to the school counselor and told him what I wished to do. He said to come back the first week of school, and he would find

9

an appropriate student. I arrived on the specified day. Both the student and his mother were there and were very eager to meet me. The counselor and I went into the classroom. The elementary school furniture was small. The mother was African-American, neatly dressed, and had a certain gleam in her eye. Her name was Charlie Mae. The student was a small boy. He was very quiet but had a certain look of hopefulness. His name was Willie. We introduced ourselves. There wasn't much conversation. Willie was enrolled in the after-school program, so we agreed that I would come and sign in with the office any afternoon I could, and I would tutor him there. They asked when I could start, and I said the next day. We agreed, and they left. I also went to talk to his teacher. I met her in the teachers' lounge. She sat rather slumped in the chair. She was sadly at the stage of burnout where many teachers, social workers, and others frequently get after years of fighting the system and not seeming to make much difference. She said that Willie basically could not read and had behavior problems as well. She obviously had very little hope or enthusiasm for what I was proposing to do. I later learned that Willie was actually considered to be the worst behavior problem in the school, and the staff essentially had a lottery betting how long I would hold out. It was in terms of weeks. Nobody ever got any money off of that lottery.

My first day after school, I met Willie, and he was very polite. However, he absolutely refused to even attempt to read. We did find certain books that he would at least open, such as *I Spy*, where a bunch of items are listed and the student is supposed to find them in the pictures. Of course, he refused to read from the list, so I would read them and he would find them, usually with ease. But when I tried to get him to find reverse the process, first identifying an object, and then asking him to find it on the list, he again refused. This went on for days. One thing we did have in common was basketball. Whenever he would completely shut down, I would suggest we go shoot some hoops on the school playground and then come back and try some more. He loved basketball and was quite good for his age, although obviously I was able to beat him. This always frustrated him, even though I was six-foot-two and he was barely five feet. I did try other measures to engage him. I asked about his family. The household consisted of two older sisters by another father, Willie's father (Wilson) and mother (Charlie Mae), and Willie. I asked him if he could draw me either a picture or a diagram of the house where lived. The picture was the typical eight-year-old's picture of a house from the outside with a window and a door. However, when I asked him to draw a floor plan or diagram of the inside of the house, he was totally incapable. Even when I guided him completely, saying, "Now, when you walk in the front door. What room do you see?" etc. he was still incapable. His father came to pick him up on a bicycle that day, so I tried to enlist his help. I asked him to draw me the floor plan of their house. He was totally unable to do it as well, although he was entirely literate. Something about the abstraction blocked him. I also had Willie draw a self-portrait (See page 15 for portrait). The one he drew of himself appears to have a huge afro, which Willie had never had at all. At least in the self-portrait he is smiling. The afro looks like it was suddenly flattened on the top, almost as if something was holding him down. His actual school photo (Found on page 16) from that year is shown alongside his drawing.

Within a couple of weeks, Willie was asking me if I could drive him home. That was definitely not within the scope of the agreement I had with the school, so I said no. One day, I visited his class during the school day and found him outside the classroom, kicking the door violently. Apparently when he became too disruptive to the rest of the class, the teacher would put him outside and he would kick the door until he either got tired or got sent to the principal's office.

I had an upcoming vacation planned for about ten days, so I told both Willie and the school that I would be away. When I returned I went to the school and was told that Willie had become so disturbed one day, he tried to run out in front of traffic. The counselor had to physically restrain him and call 911. He was considered a danger to himself and committed to a facility. The school had not heard further. I knew where he lived. It was a small, predominately black neighborhood, not far from the hospital where I was working. Not one of the huge inner city–type neighborhoods, but a smaller one with a variety of small houses, Section 8 apartments, and the stereotypical small store owned and run by Koreans. I drove there and found his mother outside of their house. She said that Willie had been released from the facility but didn't want to go back to school. He was home, so I talked to him. We had already begun to feel some rapport. He said he had not minded being in the facility at all. He was fed regularly, nobody bothered him, and they even had a basketball hoop. I asked his mother to bring Willie and meet me at the school the next day. She came as we agreed, and we talked with the principal. Luckily, on the same grounds as the school was a privately endowed school for kids with learning disabilities and behavior disorders. They had specially trained staff and much smaller student-to-teacher ratios. Neither Willie nor his mother wanted Willie to enter into that program because of that stigma of being labeled "Special ED." I talked with the director of the program and was immediately convinced that was where he needed to be. The director was an African-American woman who had never lost her hope or zeal. The students were a mixture—white, black, Hispanic, male, female, from low IQs to genius, but none of them fit in the "normal" classroom. I got Willie and his mother to agree to enroll him. The only problem was that those kids were not eligible for the after-school program, so I could not tutor Willie there. I offered to pick up Willie at his house after school and take him to the hospital education center to continue the tutoring. Willie and his mom both agreed.

My new routine involved driving to his house, taking Willie and often his sister Leslie to the hospital education center, and attempting to tutor him there. This rapidly became very challenging. When Willie decided he didn't want to study any more on any given day, he would literally get on the floor and start moaning loudly and rolling around. He even rolled out of the library several times and down the hallway. I just followed, never touching him or trying to restrain him. Eventually he would tire of this. Often it would cease as abruptly as it started, and he would get up and be ready to leave. This made it appear on one level that it was an "act," something that he did merely to get out of doing work or for attention. On another level there was real pain there, of that I was certain. I told his teachers about his behavior. Finally, one day, he flatly refused to go home.

Fortunately that day his sister was along, because he refused to leave the library and I couldn't force him to. So I left him there with his sister and made the short drive to his house to bring his mother back with me. When she got there, she told him to get up or his father would take a belt to him as soon as he got home. He got right up and we all went to his house. I couldn't see risking a repeat of that episode, so I asked if I could tutor him at home from then on. They said yes. I was the first white person who had ever been inside their house or had known them at all, other than a few government types, police, etc. In fact I later learned that Willie had been told that all white people were bad. They had no phone at all. This was before the widespread availability of cell phones. His father did part-time construction, but they were constantly broke and definitely could not afford the larger deposit people in his neighborhood were charged for phone service. So I offered to have a landline installed, which cost me almost nothing and at least gave me some ability to coordinate with them, plus to have 911 if they ever needed it. Willie's house was cluttered and filthy. His father's tools were stacked on the kitchen table. I never saw them sit down for a meal, except maybe for special events such as Thanksgiving or Christmas. Dirty clothes were piled everywhere. The single bathroom had the door off of its hinges. The bathroom sink was propped up and poorly connected to the drainpipe. There were two bedrooms, also very cluttered. We used the one where Willie slept. We would go in, and I would attempt to teach Willie to read. Of course, I had no formal training in this at all. I could see that it was a huge struggle for him. After about an hour, he was literally spent. Sometimes we would go out at that point and get something to eat. He always wanted me to drive around more while he ate in the car. I soon realized that if he reached home without finishing what he had, his sisters or whoever else was there was likely to take it from him and eat it themselves. Another time, I left him off at the park near his house, and he was walking on the sidewalk with his Happy Meal when I heard a loud sound go *pop, pop*! Everyone else in the area hit the ground, but Willie just kept on walking. A guy came staggering out of a building, obviously shot. I yelled at Willie to come get in the car. He did, and I took him home real fast and then went to the ER. The police station, EMS station, and the hospital were all within a few blocks of one another, and so I arrived at the ER almost simultaneously with EMS and police, and I helped treat the gunshot victim.

The first book Willie really showed an interest in was about Helen Keller. After days and days of practice, I felt confident that Willie could read one page flawlessly. I called his mother into the room and told Willie to go ahead. He was extremely nervous, but managed to overcome his fears and doubts for one moment. He read the page perfectly. As he finished, his mother's eyes were actually filled with tears. She was so happy and proud. Willie looked up very slowly. He was so accustomed to criticism, to being beaten down, that I really don't think he knew what to expect. She said, "He can read!" I think his feeling was more one of relief than of pride in his accomplishment. And rather than being the realization of my original "goal," this was actually barely the first step on a journey that would take all of us to places and experiences I could not ever have predicted or imagined at that moment.

Who's this stranger . . . Mike

As a second grader – nine years old, it's kind of hard to imagine a stranger which happens to be white wanting to be your Mentor. I asked myself, "What is a mentor? What is he going to be doing with me?"

At this point in my life, I felt so unloved and so unimportant. I was having so many challenges in school. I questioned myself "Why did he want to help me learn how to read?" I didn't want him in my life. I was an angry kid that just wanted to be left alone. I was so apprehensive.

I remember that day. I was in the afterschool care program when up walked my Mom to pick me up. I notice that she had this tall white man with her. My first thought was "Who is he?"

"Come here Willie. I have someone to introduce to you. This is Dr. Michael Starry. He wants to be your mentor and help you learn how to read. The Asst. Principal called and told me about him. I want you to respect him just like you do any other adult. I better not hear of you being disrespectful in any way. Do you understand me?" said his Mom. I simply replied, "Yes Ma'am".

That was the very beginning of our long relationship with Mike. As time went on, I had to learn to respect and trust him. It wasn't easy. I presented a lot of challenges to him. I'm sure he wondered many times if I was worth it. I was a nine-year-old, angry, stubborn, acting out boy who needed a lot of unconditional love.

Mike was the only white man ever excepted in our home. He would be trying to tutor me in the bedroom and they would be arguing as if he wasn't there. I'm sure there were times when he couldn't believe his eyes or ears. The witnessing of my mother's drug addiction and having to work on her when she would be beaten and have to come to the Emergency Room. He was always available to help those in need, especially my Mom. So many times, he helped her through rough financial times. With Mike in my life I had a much better chance of being a better person. I know he did what he did because he cared so much for me and my family.

CHAPTER 2

My Background

Everyone views the world through their own prism, formed by their background and experiences. I am no exception. In my case both sides of my family, paternal and maternal have been in Texas over 150 years. My paternal grandfather had a farm in central Texas, that is where my father was born in 1923. At that time, the farm had no running water. Water was drawn from the well, and they also had an outhouse for a toilet. There was no electricity, kerosene lamps provided light, and a wood-burning stove provided for cooking and warmth. Life was hard compared to what we have today. They worked the land six days a week, taking off Sunday to go to church. My grandfather was a huge man and very strong. He was aware that if he had ever hit anyone, he could seriously harm or even kill them. As a result, he was one of the gentlest men imaginable. Even though they were isolated, my grandparents made certain that my father attended school. He graduated high school and was helping out on the farm when a college scout came to evaluate a teammate that had played on the high school football team alongside him. The teammate suggested to the scout that he evaluate my father while he was there. He did and offered my father a full football scholarship to Southwestern University in Georgetown, Texas. My father rode his horse off to college. Shortly thereafter, World War II began. My father enlisted in the Navy and over the next few years went all over North Africa,

Europe, and finally the South Pacific, experiencing parts of the world and cultures that he never dreamed of as a boy.

Both World War II and the post war economic prosperity had interesting and uneven effects on the status of blacks in the United States. When we sent so many young men to fight overseas, there was a need for increased production at home to keep the military supplied. The resulting "manpower" shortage was filled with women (Rosie the Riveter), as well as blacks who migrated from the rural south to urban areas in the south and north. This was a liberating experience for both women and blacks. It was the first time that women and blacks had been economically empowered in this country. In addition, blacks made some progress in other areas during the war, such as the Tuskegee airmen. President Truman integrated the military by executive order in 1948. But racial discrimination was still the norm in this country, especially in the rural south. (Read about Emmet Till, Medgar Evers, among others.)

My father returned from the war, went back to college where got his degree, and also met my mother. They moved to Houston, Texas. This is where I grew up. Even though my parents were not wealthy, we still had a maid that came weekly. Her name was Emma. She was somewhat older. I really loved her. When she would go to the store, I would ride with her in the back of the bus. It never really occurred to me why.

Such is the nature of privilege. Those in any society who possess it often take it completely for granted. There were really no black people in my neighborhood or in my life. My father had kept the family farm and had continued to work on it part-time till his late seventies. Frequently he would hire blacks to help out. He always treated them with respect, being concerned only that they did their work, not with the color of their skin. They returned his respect. I never heard my parents express bigotry or hatred towards blacks or any other groups. Of course now, in retrospect, I can see where some of their opinions or attitudes, as well as some of my own, contained elements of racism.

As I entered college, I began to have more interaction with blacks, particularly as I loved playing basketball and would play pickup games wherever I could. I also dropped out of college for nine months and worked construction to make money to finish school. Here I was working alongside black workers and white workers as well. The crews tended to be segregated along racial lines. Many of the white workers felt little in common with me, as I was a college student; in their thinking I was in a different class in society (somewhat true), and thought I was better than them (largely their own projections). Sometimes the white crews would try to make me look foolish or fail in some way. I found the black crews to be more accepting. As long as I did my share of the work, there was generally no problem.

The first black person that I can say was a true friend was in medical school. Wassel was older than the average medical student, having already achieved a PhD. He also already had a family, a wife, and three children. For some reason I had always had a sense of not really fitting in, of being more of an outside observer than a member of any group. He was in a similar situation, so we identified with each other somewhat and became best friends. My parents had a house on a lake north of Houston and a boat, so when I learned that Wassel (and especially his wife) liked to fish, I invited them up for the weekend. I went ahead on Friday and they were coming on Saturday. They were late and when they got there, I could tell that something was wrong. It turned out that some sheriff had pulled them over. They were doing nothing wrong other than being black in an area that was white. Wassel was smart enough to know that he was in a no-win situation. He knew that the sheriff would have taken any excuse to arrest him. With his young children watching, this PhD sat there and stayed quiet. I felt so bad. He assured me that this was nothing new, he certainly didn't hold me responsible in any way, and he suggested that we go ahead and enjoy the rest of the weekend, which we did. But the impression still lingers for me as strongly. (As a postscript, as I was writing this book, I contacted Wassel for his input. Amazingly to me, he didn't seem to remember the incident that I had previously mentioned. He told me it was so commonplace for such a thing to happen to blacks that he would never recall every single incident in relation to racial discrimination.)

As I had continued in life, I had a number of close black friends. But all of them were educated and mostly professional.

Willie was different. He had so many barriers he had to overcome. Of course, there is racism. There is also a huge class difference. In addition, he had both genetic predisposition and the environment putting him at high risk for drug abuse, physical abuse, and so many other negatives. Willie's world was almost a polar opposite of mine.

As time went on, I learned more and more about his family. Charlie Mae was a decent student in high school and actually ran on the track team. After graduation she got a job at a retail store. Then she married some guy, and he got her hooked on cocaine. He was also abusive. They eventually parted ways, and she got together with the father of Willie's two half sisters. He was also into drugs. She had lost her job. Lastly, she got together with the present man, who *also* sold drugs and was physically abusive. He had multiple arrests, including aggravated assault, and had supposedly killed someone and had weapons in the house. Willie's maternal grandmother, who seemed like a sweet lady, had killed two men—one for molesting one of her daughters. Charlie Mae also had multiple arrests and had done time. Both Charlie Mae and Willie's grandmother told me that at one time or another, they had each made plans to kill Wilson. Sometimes, when Charlie Mae and Wilson would get into fights, Willie would run to his grandmother's house and spend the night. So where were the authorities? They knew. They were just totally overwhelmed, as they admitted to me later. When Charlie Mae got pregnant with Willie, she was using cocaine heavily. To her credit, as soon as she found out that she was pregnant, she quit cold turkey and was clean for the remainder of her pregnancy. But during those first eight to ten weeks or so, Willie was awash in cocaine in utero. Then he was born into a culture of drugs and abuse. Willie's father, Wilson, also used drugs and alcohol, sold drugs, had multiple arrests and had killed someone. I certainly did not appreciate at the time, nor can I to this day really fully imagine the damage that all of that had done.

My Life Story

Early Years

My name is Willie Charles Bentley. I was born in Jackson Hospital, Miami, FL. My mother raised me in South Miami, Florida – Lee Park, St. John AME Church, Good & Plenty Store, Mt. Olive Missionary Baptist Church and on and on. During my early childhood I – about 6 years old – lived in my Grandma's three bedroom blue and white house. There were about twenty family members living there. My Mom and her sisters and their children all lived together in this one house. The children slept on the floor and on-air mattresses – boys in one room and the girls in the other. It was uncomfortable by I enjoyed being with all my family members especially my cousins, Larry, Patrick, Harry, Sheba, and of course, my sisters. We would play on the air mattresses like they were trampolines. It was a lot of fun -being a kid playing with my cousins, non-stop. Every Sunday we had to go to Church – Mt. Olive Baptist Church. My Grandma didn't play that no church stuff.

Eventually, my mom was able to move out on her own. She qualified for Section 8 housing so she was now able to take care of us. We moved just two houses down from my Grandma's house. Now It was just my mom, my sisters, my Dad and me.

When I got old enough to go to school I attended Ludlam Elementary. I remember my sister Leslie walking me to class to leave me in a room full of kids. I was so scared. I didn't know the kids so I acted out. I would scream, throw myself on the floor, cry and yell "don't leave me... I don't know these people." I was only used to being around my sister. My teacher had to call my sister back to the classroom several times to calm me down because I was crying as if someone were trying to kidnap me. Come to find out I had one of the sweetest teachers at Ludlam.

The next school year comes and it's time to go to school. I'm set for 2nd grade. I get to the school and began to look at the boards with the teacher's names and the names of students. I look for my name and it's not under any of the second -grade class lists. I asked the teacher at the board. "where is my name." It was pointed out to me that I had been retained and was shown my name on the first -grade list. I repeated first grade again where most of the students knew me. I was told that my mom, Charlie Mae Bentley, requested that I stay back and I didn't even know it.

They used to crack jokes about my mom's burned spot on her neck. You see, my mom got into a fight with a lady in our neighborhood and she threw "pot ash" on her neck and left a serious burn. That scar became a permanent reminder of the incident. To this day I don't know who did it to her. I never had a chance to ask her about it. It's probably for the best. I don't think I wanted to know. . . it caused me too much pain. I wouldn't want to *catch a case* because of it.

I couldn't take it when kids talked about my Mom. Everybody knows that you don't talk about someone's Mom. I just wanted to him to be quiet. He wouldn't so we began to fight. I threw the first punch. We are swinging at each other. The teacher came over to stop us. When she found out that I started the fight, I was sent to sit outside the classroom on the bench. Here I sat outside fuming but I knew I needed to get back in class. My Mom and Dad didn't play when it came to school, I would be in double trouble. So, I started beating on the windows, air conditioning grill, and even the door. I was just angry and wanted to hit something. to get my anger out. The teacher wouldn't let me in. Shortly after this incident I met Dr. Michael Starry. You see, my mom was told about this Doctor that wanted to tutor a child that was having trouble with Reading. My mom introduced him to me.

I wasn't a good reader. When I would read and get corrected and I would get distracted and mad. It was easy for me to get in trouble in school. I would always get kicked out of class. When I would get sent out of class I would do my usual- beat on the air-condition grill to disrupt the class.

One day this pretty black young lady came walking down the hallway. She stopped and told me to stop hitting that air conditioning grill. I quickly told her "no". She told me to get down from up there and come talk to her. So, I got down from up there and came down so we could talk. I sat on the bench with her and began to tell her my problems. I shared that the kids were teasing me because I didn't know how to read and about my mama. I didn't have a clue who she was. Later I found out she was the Behavior Management Teacher for this special program in the school. She later became important in assisting with getting me placed me in the special program for children with problems like mine. Her name was Ms. Combs.

My anger was sometimes uncontrollable. I remember this one day I ran out of the school. I was headed home – mad. I just wanted to leave. I was tired of that class – the teacher and the students. I went running down the sidewalk toward the traffic light. The school's security saw me and thought I was going to run in the street in front of a car. I could hear them calling me ..." WILLIE! WILLIE! WILLIE!" The school's counselor saw me and began calling me back. They threatened to call the police. I turned around and finally went back to the school. I didn't want to do but I knew I had to.

The school called my mom and she immediately called Mike, my new tutor. After all, he was a Doctor. He rushed to the school and talked to the Principal about the incident. After their conference, he agreed to take me to a psychiatric hospital in Hialeah for a safety evaluation. The arrangements were made and off we went. When I arrived to the hospital the people in the window got my name from Mike. They later called us back and began to get information regarding the incident that happened at school. After evaluating my answers, they decided that I was possibly a danger to myself or others. Today they call it Baker-Act. I had to stay there for three days. Believe it or not, after I got over the fear of this place, I began to enjoy it. It wasn't that bad... I sort of liked it. Kids who were there had problems just like me. We would sit in group and talk about our problems with the counselors. I was medicated and It calmed me down a little, but I still don't think it helped.

After leaving the hospital I had to return to school. It was weird. I wasn't sure how the students would react to me. When I got back I was told I would need to go with this Psychologist to take all these tests. She would come and get me from the classroom. I would have to answer questions about reading and math along with questions about my feelings. I remember after the test was completed there was a big meeting. My Mom and Mike were at the school. My Mom and Mike were told about the benefits of a program in the school that would be help me with my anger. The program was called T.O.P.S. They were excited about the new class I would be going to especially because it was still in the school, smaller classes, therapists, special tutoring, group counseling, etc.

After the meeting was over they came to pick me up from After Care. I was told that they were at this meeting to talk about what the test results said and to discuss what was best for me. They explained that this program (TOPS) would help me become a better reader and also help me with my anger. They shared that I was going to be placed in this program for children with severe anger issues like mine. I would have classes with about 10 – 15 students or less. Then, they reminded me that the lady I talked to that day when I was angry, Ms. Combs, worked in that program.

I was reluctant about changing my class but as time passed I began to like it. We would have holiday shows every year and I remember singing the Christmas songs that Ms. Mincey taught us. She would make us practice until we knew the songs. Our parents would be invited to come to the program and watch us perform. Santa would bring all the children toys we selected.

One year, I wore a black tuxedo. I felt so special and less shy. I would just be singing. My mom came but she had a black eye. She was wearing sun glasses so no one would notice. She wouldn't miss the program even though she had been fighting with my dad. I know she didn't have it when I left for school that morning. I knew what happened … Another fight! My mom would come to everything we had – field days, holiday and end-of-year programs. She was so involved regardless of what else was going on.

MOM

My mother was my biggest fan. She didn't miss any of my events or activities. Even when she was on drugs or had a black eye she was the #1 Mom in my eyes – it didn't matter what people use to say. I would be playing in South Miami Park and on the sidelines, I could hear her yelling, "Run Boy Run!" That lady was always there. Sometimes, I would get surprise visits from Mike. If he wasn't too busy he would stop by to watch me play. He thought I was pretty good.

My first remembrance of my mom using drugs was when I was around 7or 8 years old. She and her friends were in the room. I could hear them laughing and talking. When they would come out I could see that something was going on. One time I went in and saw traces of the white powder. It was then that I realized they were snorting cocaine, that was her drug of choice. When she was using she would go to herself – get mellow, calm, and quiet. She would play cards with me, dance, and get very playful. Regardless of her condition, she would always have food for us to eat.

My Dad would come home drunk –Yes, he had a drinking problem. That's when all hell would break out. He would get abusive, especially at night. She would accuse him of not being able to perform sexually, cheating with the ladies in the neighborhood, or she would withhold sex from him. He would deny it, get angry and the fight would begin. I witnessed him on several occasions hitting my mom. She would be screaming and I would go see what was going on. I remember one night she was in bed with me, avoiding him, and he came in the room and hit her right in front of my face. Sometimes, I would hear her crying- She would try to not let me hear. He would yell at her to hush but I would hear the awful sounds as I lay in my bed – glass breaking, banging. When I would get up to go in he would tell me to "take my ass back to my room". I would tell him to get off of her. I felt so helpless. I still do. Why couldn't I save her???

I hated coming home after dark because I knew they would get into a fight. I would get beatings from being out at night. I just didn't want to be there. On the weekends, I would always find friends to spend the night at their house or the entire weekend.

It was so hard going to school every day knowing my mom wasn't safe to be home alone by herself. I had to be a young man at an early age so my mom would keep me. If I would have told anyone about what was going on at my house at school I wonder would they have been able to help me and my mom out. This big family filled with problems made me feel like nobody loved or cared about how this could be messing up my life. My life was so rough growing up as a kid. I would try to go to school and stay focused, get back home and people talking about my mom, I just wished I was dead before I kill someone and throw my life away. Growing up in the ghetto, you don't have to many chances of making it in life. You are going through pain at home and not telling nobody. You just holding this pain in for so long, so long, you just wish it was over- it gets to be too much. I was young and realizing things at a very young age. You feel like nobody loves you. Just see what I would go through every day.

DAD

My dad didn't like Mike for nothing in this world and I still don't know why. As a kid, my dad had a bad background but he kept a good job. He had five boys from four different women. My dad used to give me money but never came to support me at any of my sports events or school activities. He always showed me hard love. My dad used to beat my ass so much. I felt like he didn't love me like my other brothers. He never came out to support me even though I was great at every sport I played.

When my dad lost his Mom, everything changed about him. It's crazy how your dad wouldn't reach out to his own son like how his son reached out to him to make sure everything was alright with him. I remember when my dad took me to help him work at this lady house – putting flowers in her yard. She had three dogs. Dad, I also remember you and my cousin used to get your boys so they can get to know each other and the family. NO matter what, I really enjoyed being with the family.

Dad, one thing we have in common - You and I both know how it feels to lose a Mother.

He and my Mom had an abusive relationship. I blamed him for her death. She endured so many beating that I felt eventually killed her. She had a brain bleed. He started talking to my mom's good friend after her death. Some say they were already in a relationship. He moved in with her and left me in the apartment that we lived in with my mom. I was lost and confused -a minor can't stay in an apartment without an adult.

SISTERS

I have two sisters, Jackie and Leslie. My oldest sister, Jackie, reminds me a lot of my mother. She is mouthy, drink, talk trash, loud, sold and used drugs, shot dice, wild, played basketball, been in jail more than once. She would stand up against any man. I would sometimes think . . . she's crazy. She was not a girly girl. She experienced abusive relationships. She gave my mom the most hell. She dropped out of school in the 12th grade. Wow! I always felt I had to protect her.

At the time of my mom's death, Jackie was incarcerated on a drug charge but she was allowed to attend the funeral, with supervision. Two weeks after the funeral, she was released. She stayed in the apartment with me and in no time her boyfriend moved in. They began their abusive relationship. They fought all the time – verbally and physically. Here I was living in the apartment with them trying to protect my sister. One day, after I got into an argument her boyfriend, I was kicked out. My clothes, my Jordan's and my bed were thrown out in the streets, everything I owned. Why would she do this to me? I had nowhere to go. *"She threw me out to be with her nigger...!"*

My other sister is Leslie. She has one child. She is quiet, mellow and much more reserved. She is a lot like me. No drama. She is married but financially struggling to get on her feet. She is the church girl. She has to stay with her husband's family until times get better.

MIKE . . . My Mentor. . . My Family . . . My Friend

There were times when I was younger when I use to wish I was dead before I met Mike. My life was always filled with drama – the fighting, drug abuse, being evicted, etc. There was no peace in my home. I just wanted to give up on everything. Until the day I met this gentle giant, Mike. He opened my eyes to want more out of life and to get out of the hood. He showed me what was possible. I look at Michael Starry as my role model. Somebody that gave me something else to look forward to, to try something different from what I already knew.

I loved playing sports, especially basketball and so did he. Mike and I would shoot hoops when he thought I needed a break during our tutoring sessions. When I became frustrated he would say . . . "Let's go shot some hoops. You're tired. Let's take a break!"

He came to tutor me in reading because I hated reading out loud because the students use to laugh at me when I messed up a word. I would then get really mad and wouldn't read any more. But the more Mike and I kept working hard together so I could get better at reading. I started to read a little better.

Together, Mike and I worked hard through the years to help me become a better reader. I slowly started to read a little better. It took time and patience with me because I had a short fuse in my head that would make me say words that I didn't mean to say. I thank the man above for putting this special *white* man in my life even though he was different from my kind of people. I loved Mike like he was part of my own family but he wasn't. He would take me away from all my problems that I had to see every day. That's the only time I was really happy, excited, joyful, and proud of myself for earning everything with a smile on my face. He did things that my parents couldn't do for me because every cent my mom had went on the bills, food and drugs. I'm not sure where I'd be right now without Mikes influence on my life. He has tried to push me to be a better person and now a better man.

Mike was introduced to my crazy world early in our relationship. He got a chance to witness the dysfunction of my family and neighborhood. It didn't stop him for trying to help me learn how to read. He did so much for me and my family. When my mom was going to be evicted he agreed to pay the rent monthly. This act of kindness lasted for many years. He would do it with the understanding that she couldn't use drugs and that my Dad couldn't stay there because of the domestic violence history. She never followed it. He was always disappointed. The drugs always won.

C H A P T E R   3

The New Routine

It was the fall so of course that meant football. I began to go to Willie's practice sometimes and watch. Athletics play a huge role in the lives of black youth. Many of them see athletics as their best hope of success, although the statistics say otherwise. The more athletic kids are definitely viewed and treated differently. Willie was small but actually was quite athletic. Even at that age he was quite accurate throwing a football and in basketball could make three-pointers with good consistency. One day I was watching practice and the coach sent the team to run a lap around the field. A toddler had wandered out onto the field. The entire team ran over him, knocked him over and left him crying. Willie was the only one that looked back. When he saw the child he came back, picked him up and carried him to the child's mother, who had not been paying the least attention. Then he ran and rejoined the team. I was the only one that noticed.

As I spent more and more time with Willie, he began to look to me or guidance. This put me in a strange and sometimes uncomfortable situation. I was not sure how the values I held would serve him in his environment. On issues like fighting, I was personally opposed, but I realized that my values might actually put him in jeopardy. Another was corporal punishment. That was not part of my experience growing up. I came up with a strategy that I thought worked. I described how when football player went on the field they wore pads and helmets. When they were off the field they wore regular clothes. I suggested that when he was in his environment that he put on the "uniform" that would serve him best there. But when he was out in regular (white) society that he should change uniforms, including his language that would best serve him there. I think he got it. One day as I was leaving his house his father was sitting on the front steps and I bent over to say goodbye to him. Willie poked his head over my far shoulder and with me safely in between him and his father Willie said "Doc says you aren't supposed to hit me anymore." There was an uncomfortable moment. His father looked at me almost quizzically wondering what I would say. I deflected it somewhat, saying something like "What was the reason for him to hit you?" Willie said whatever it was and then I said something like "If you mind your parents then it shouldn't be an issue." I wasn't very happy with my response. On the other hand, I was regularly going into another man's house and teaching his son. It was touchy.

Willie was tremendously curious to find out where I lived. The irony was that I lived right across the street from his school. That first Christmas my family came to visit. The day I had to take my parents to the airport I was running late and had Willie with me in the car. The only way I could make is was to take him with me, which meant he would finally know where I lived.

I let his family know right away that Willie now knew where I lived. We mutually tried to set some rules so that Willie wouldn't just come over all of the time. He didn't follow the rules very well. One Saturday morning the doorbell rang and when I looked through the peephole and there was Willie. I didn't answer. He rang it again. I didn't answer. Then he sat down on the landing and started sobbing.

What was I supposed to do? I opened the door. He was instantly happy. My townhouse had a swimming pool and he wanted me to teach him to swim. So I did. At first he made it on pure athletic ability and determination. We stayed in the shallow end for days. He kept wanting to go in the deep end. I told him that he had to be comfortable going the length of the pool in the shallow end first. He virtually willed himself across, holding his breath the whole way. We kept at it and he was finally actually swimming, not just thrashing. Then we went to the deep end. I think it really came to him that it was over his head. There was some momentary panic. I saw it and told him that it was no different than swimming across the shallow end. Plus I would be there. The trust he showed was truly amazing. He pushed off and swam confidently across the pool. He never had any fear of the water again. Several months later Willie and his cousin Larry went with me to some friends' house who had a pool. Willie and Larry wanted to go in the pool. That pool had a sloped bottom that got deep pretty quickly. They both got in and Larry started walking to the deep end. Suddenly it was over his head and he completely panicked. It all happened really fast. Larry was actually drowning. Willie swam over to him to pull him out and Larry did what drowning people often do, he grabbed Willie around the neck and pulled him under. Now they were both drowning. I jumped in without even removing my shoes. I pulled them both to the shallow end. They were both coughing up water. Willie was fairly calm but Larry was still panicking. It took several minutes for things to calm down. I just couldn't believe how fast it occurred. I had no idea that Larry could not swim yet was willing to get in the pool and actually go to where it was over his head.

Later that spring I asked Willie one Sunday if he would like to go to the beach. He said yes, and asked if we could take some friends. I said okay and he asked how many? I half-jokingly said as many as you can fit in my car. I had a big Lincoln Town Car. Twelve kids later Willie and I set off for the beach. I'm lucky we didn't get pulled over. When we got to the beach they all scrambled out of the car to get in the water. Shortly thereafter about half of them came running back. "It tastes salty!" they yelled. They had never been in the ocean. I told them that was how it was supposed to be and they went back in. Although there were only thirteen of them they were easy to keep track of; they were the only black kids at the entire beach. They had a good time although there were some boundary issues. If other (white) kids had a ball or a sand pail these kids would just go up and start playing with them. I had some angry parents, but no fights or anything. They never fought in my presence as long as I can remember. As they grew older that changed. There was violence, robberies, assaults, even shootings. Some of the shootings were quite serious, some fatal.

By the end of that first school year Willie was doing really well. He was making all A's and B's in school. He received several awards. He still had occasional behavioral problems, mainly episodes of extreme stubbornness. Summer school was offered and it was certainly a better alternative to sitting at home. He was liking school much better now, so it was not difficult to get him to go.

FRIENDS … WHERE ARE THEY NOW?

Growing up in the ghetto of South Miami I had a lot of friends but there were some that were very close to me and continue to be to this day even though our paths have taken on many different turns. Their lives mirrored many of the struggles that I experienced. Our parents were poor, alcoholics, drug addicts, abused, uneducated, incarcerated, just to name a few. We all had dreams but they were never fulfilled.

As youngsters, we all loved to play sports especially football and basketball. We would compete, get angry for losing, fight each other and still remained friends. I, especially, hated to lose. Some of us went to Ludlam Elem together. It was as though we were a brotherhood. Our lives revolved around Lee Park where we were free to safely play sports and stay out of trouble.

Mike was really good about accepting my friends. He never judged any of them. He would take us to his house and let us get in the pool and have a good time. You see, there were no pools in our neighborhood. We would go get pizzas, McDonalds, or Burger King. We would go to Game Stop, or to the movies. He just wanted them to know he cared. He simply wanted to be able to help them experience a good time with having to financially stress their parents to do so. Mike has a big heart!

I remember once when we were getting ready to go out and I invited a few of my friends to go. One of my friends wanted to really go but he shared that he had no shoes to wear. He also shared that his siblings didn't have any. Mike took me to their house and got all their sizes. We then left and went to the store and bought all of them shoes.

As you can imagine our lives didn't go as planned. As we've grown older, we have met many challenges trying to grow up as young me. Without stable homes and proper guidance, we've made bad choices which landed us incarcerated or with many encounters with law enforcement. Offenders of the law. Some have moved away while some of us are still trying to figure it out- in and out of jail.

Timmy & Robert went to Ludlam Elem. They were also in the program for for children with special emotional needs. They were raised by their dad who was very old and couldn't read. When my Mom was living she would help watch them and help their dad him with reading. You see, many said that their Mom deserted them for the streets when they were very young. When their dad passed away they struggled to stay in school. Today, they are constantly in and out of jail for *robbery and selling drugs*. Timmy is out now but I don't know for how long.

Jontavis and I spent a lot of time together. I spent many nights at his house, playing video games and he stayed at mine. He, too, is now locked up on a *capital murder charge.*

When **Big Ben** and I were teenagers we would sneak out of the house and take his mom's car to go to clubs. I spent the night, played video games and he also spent nights at my house too. He was always there for me. *He was my #1. He always had my back if I needed him.* Now he is locked up on a gun charge.

Lil Danny was also a very good friend. My #1. We use to played chase and get on top of the park's center's roof. We would also get chased by the police. We beat up people for fun - no reason. He moved to South Carolina around the age of 18. I lost touch with him.

CHAPTER 4

Hitting the Wall

My second year with Willie, things continued to go well. He was still applying himself both in school and in our tutoring sessions. I was becoming hopeful that if he continued on this trajectory, he could go to college or become whatever he wished.

The CEO of the hospital where I worked and I had some long-shared interests, one of which was basketball. Wayne had two sons, one a little older than Willie, and one just younger. I had Willie with me one day when I went by Wayne's house. Wayne had a half-court basketball court and Willie gravitated toward it and started shooting. The son just younger than Willie saw him and started shooting baskets with him. They were so compatible with each other, this black kid from an inner-city environment who had never known a white guy until he met me, and this white kid who had never been near a ghetto. Up until then. Over the next few years, they continued to interact so easily. When it was Bring Your Child to Work Day. Willie asked if I would take him with me to the hospital. I did, and he and this boy had a great time together, actually going into the OR and watching open-heart surgery. Wayne invited me and Willie to go with them to a professional basketball game and we used the hospital's box seats. They began to invite Willie every year to his son's birthday party. But slowly, subtly at first and then glaringly obvious, the profound differences in their situations exerted its influence.

While Wayne's was a stable home with two parents and no violence, Willie's home was increasingly unstable. One night, Willie's parents were drinking and doing cocaine and got into one of their many physical fights. The fight landed them both in the hospital. Child protective services was contacted and called in to find temporary placement. They were looking for a relative to place the child with, but their policy was that the relative could not have a felony charge. I was told that they went through over a dozen relatives, until they gave up and put them with a foster family temporarily. I was not given any contact with him as I did not have any official standing. After about a week, Charlie Mae was discharged and took them back. This type of incident was not isolated and kept Willie in a state of constant chaos and terror. Willie also seemed to lack a certain drive. He would respond to my efforts to some extent, but I could not seem to summon that drive from within him. It was as if he did not truly accept that he would be able to positively affect his own future. I tried many small things to try to show him differently. As I mentioned before, the house was filthy. I offered to at least clean and paint his room. He took very little interest in it, I and some of my friends did most of the work. One guy from the neighborhood did seem to take an interest and asked if he could help out. We said sure. When we were finished, the guy asked how much I was going to pay him. The room looked really good but Willie did not thank any of us or really seem to care. Of course, this was my idea, not his.

Willie had become very familiar to all of the staff in the ER. One day I was doing some work in the hot attic of my townhome and become rather dizzy and weak. I went over to the ER to have them check me out just to be on the safe side. Within thirty minutes, Willie arrived on the bike I had bought for him and walked right into the room where I was. I was fairly amazed at how the word had spread to him so quickly, and also how deep his concern was. He really needed to see that I was okay.

The next Christmas, my parents came to visit again. They had gotten to know Willie also. Of course we had a tree with gifts under it, some of them for him. Christmas morning, he arrived bright and early. He was eager to open presents. Not only those that were for him, but he got joy out of seeing all of us giving and sharing. My mother opened one present—I have no recollection of what it was or who it was from—but she threw her hands up in surprise. She wasn't that near to Willie, but he obviously flinched reflexively. I saw it, and so did she. Our gazes met and there was a certain sadness.

A couple of grades later, Willie began to wane in enthusiasm for the work. I mentioned it to Charlie Mae, and she said she would talk to him. He was still showing signs of laziness, much preferring to watch television than to do homework. How do you instill the desire to learn in a child who lived day to day in an environment where things like an education, hard work, and deferred goals were not valued? He saw only the end result with me, not of the years of work that had gone into achieving what I had. Plus I was white. He had often told me that he no longer perceived me as white, and I feel he was sincere. But at the same time, his personal worldview was that people of his type, meaning poor and black, just never made it. I was watching Barack Obama come up in politics, and one day I had Willie and five of his friends in the car. This was probably in 2005. I asked if any of them knew who Obama was. Not one did. I asked them if they thought that the country was ready for a black to be President. They all said no. I asked them one more question: What did each of them expect to be doing in five years from then? They were all about sixteen at the time. Almost in unison they told me they didn't really expect to be alive by then. They were serious.

One night at about 11:00 p.m., I got a call from Willie. He never called that late. He said I need to come over right away. I was there within a few minutes. As I pulled up, both Willie and Leslie jumped into the back seat of my Lincoln. It was an ugly scene. The police were already there. Charlie Mae was in the doorway, obviously high, and screaming at the top of her lungs that she wanted to throw lye in Wilson's eyes and blind him. She was being restrained by her oldest daughter, who was sobbing and pleading with her to stop. Wilson was at a distance, behind one of the police cars. I got out of my car and went to speak with one of the officers, who happened to be female. I asked her what had started this. She said they didn't know. I asked what they were planning to do and she said they were going to have Wilson leave and stay somewhere else for the night. I said I thought that was totally inadequate, that it did not appear to be a safe environment and that we all knew this was not the first such incident, nor would it be the last. She looked at me and said, "What exactly would you like for us to do?"

I stammered a response such as, "Get family services involved."

She looked at me again and said, "This has been going on for a long time. It will probably continue to go on, and there is nothing we can really do." I went back to my car and told Willie and Leslie that Wilson had gone and they needed to go back in the house. The looks on their faces from that moment still haunt me. When they had first climbed in the car, they were afraid. Leslie was tearful. They sat so quietly, almost as if nobody noticed them, then they could go home with me. When I went to tell them that Wilson had gone and they needed to go back inside, the looks changed to ones more of pleading, then to resignation that things were just going to keep being the same. They got out of the car wordlessly, and the officer took them inside. They never looked back. I felt as I had truly let them down with my response.

The next Christmas, I was going to Houston where all of my family was. I told Willie way in advance, so that he wouldn't be taken by surprise. He asked if he could go. I thought about it and decided that if his family approved of it, I would take him along. They had no problem at all with him going. He had never been in an airplane, so there was some anxiety, but everything went fine. I stayed at my parents' house and Willie stayed at my sisters' house. She had a spare bedroom, and although it was not far from my parents', her neighborhood had more kids. He fit in fine. He helped out around the house, kept his room neat, and never complained about a thing. It almost never snows in Houston, but magically, Christmas Eve, there was solid snowfall. Enough to have snowball fights and build a snowman.

I had constantly tried to infuse elements of black history and culture into his tutoring. I tried to find things that might spark interest in him. Of course, I tried all kinds of works about and by Dr. Martin Luther King, Jr., W.E.B. Du Bois, James Baldwin, and

Nelson Mandela. I found an excellent resource on the history of the Blues and got the music to accompany it. Nothing seemed to really stimulate his mind into that state of creativity, of hopefulness and faith in the future. I saw a flyer for an African drumming workshop at the university and signed us up. True, he was the only child in the workshops but he refused to even try. That year I attended another performance of African drummers. It was fantastic. By coincidence I was at a park the next weekend and there they were, in the pavilion right next to where I was. I walked over and talked with them. Willie was just starting in a summer session, and I asked two of the drummers if they would be willing to come teach a class, if I paid them. They accepted, so we did it. Many of the students participated eagerly, to the point that they put on a performance at the end of the six-week term which was videotaped. Again, however, Willie would not participate.

I began to notice a lot of things that were like we were living in different worlds, separate realities. For example, credit cards, ATM cards, and checks. They were like magic to Willie. When he would ask for something and I would say either I didn't have any money on me or it was too expensive, he would say, "Just use your card." He truly did not grasp that a bill would come later and it would have to be paid. Likewise, after a few years, I moved from the townhouse to a larger house. At this point, Willie was spending a lot of time with me, so when the movers came, he was there. We drove over to the new house and he went through it. He came to the master suite, which was fairly large, with two walk-in closets, two sinks, a separate shower and hot tub, etc. "This is my room!" he said. He had never spent a single night at my house, and would not for many years, although he repeatedly asked to. But he was serious. I guess it was like a fantasy, but it also showed a more profound disconnect in his mind in how people actually achieve things in life.

I also tried to educate him in certain areas of life skills, such as budgeting, saving money, etc. Of course, in his own personal life experience, none of these were realities, and I seemed unable to make them so. One thing I began to notice often was an internal disconnect regarding his mother. He began not wanting her to attend school functions. She was often either high or hungover. She was also show-ing signs of deterioration from the ongoing physical abuse. Willie loved his mother deeply, and I learned later that Willie felt he failed his mother by not killing his dad. But now, she embarrassed him. He always asked me to go to his school in place of her. I continued to be respectful of Charlie Mae, but if I pushed the issue of including her, he would just decide not to go at all.

Wayne Brackin & Sons

One day while visiting with Mike he invited me to go to a meeting with him. He explained he had to meet with Mr. Wayne Brackin. He shared that Mr. Brackin had a son that was close to my age who loved to play sports as much as I did. I was eager to go with him. On the car ride I asked more questions in anticipation of meeting a possibly new friend.

Mike told me that Mr. Wayne Bracket was the CEO South Miami Hospital at the time. He later became the COO of Baptist Health Systems. He had two sons, Cyrus and Jeffrey.

As we arrived to the house I noticed that we were parking across the street from Gulliver Academy, the private prestigious school. It was a big beautiful single-story home with a golf cart, motorcycles, basketball court, swimming pool and two *big* dogs. All I could say to myself after seeing all of these things was "WOW". I couldn't believe my eyes.

As I entered the home I met the Brackin family. Everyone made me feel right at home. I instantly struck a conversation with Cyrus. We talked about all kind of things and he invited me to come outside to play on the basketball court. We jelled instantly. His family treated me like I was a family member. I felt so comfortable around them. They didn't judge me because of where I came from or because I was so different. I could tell they had a lot of money but it didn't matter.

As time went on, Cyrus and I played basketball at Lee Park in South Miami. His brother, Jeffrey, coached us for a season. To this day, Cyrus is the only person (black or white) that ever invited me to a birthday party...ever. He always remembered to invite me to his parties. Super cool dude!

Over the years, however, we've lost touch with each other. I haven't seen him in years but I know that when I see him again we will be able to rekindle our relationship with no problems. I heard Cyrus finished high school and went on to play basketball in college while I continued to face more of life's challenges -STRUGGLING.

Our lives were so vastly different. I have a lot of respect for him. I'm glad I met him.

- A Trip of a Lifetime . . . **HOUSTON, TEXAS**

When I was 9 years old Mike surprised me and took me to Houston, Texas to spend Christmas with his family. I was never so excited in all my life. You see, I'd never flown on an airplane nor had I been in an airport I was in awe of all of the sights. It was like I was in another world. I was also very scared to get on the plane but I had to trust him. The plane was so big. Looking through the window and watching the plane take off was really scary. The sounds and the bumping. When we got up in the sky everything was like little squares. After several hours of flying we finally landed. We finally made it to Houston, Texas safe. I met his parents and they greeted me like I was one of their children. You see, I met them in Miami when they would come and visit Mike. For the first time in my life I felt like I was a part of a real family and it was Christmastime.

I woke up to my favorite breakfast – *bacon, eggs and grits*. I could smell that bacon. I didn't know *white people* could cook.

I saw snow for the very first time. It felt crunchy. I opened my mouth to taste it. It tasted like frozen water. I picked up some and put it in a bowl and placed it in the freezer. I was trying to save it.

It was during this visit, I discovered there was no Santa Claus. Here's why . . . I went to the mall with the family and showed Mike asked me what I wanted for Christmas. So of course, I showed him all the things I wanted. I didn't expect to get them. I figured maybe I would get a few things as gifts from Mike and his family. When I woke up on Christmas morning I couldn't believe my eyes. My eyes were stretched wide open in disbelief. I was speechless. I had everything I pointed out to them in the mall. I didn't tell Santa all those things. What a surprise! It was truly the best Christmas I could remember.

That trip was the best trip ever. I am a boy from the ghetto who got to really enjoy a White Christmas. I really enjoyed myself with Mike's family. I didn't want to leave such an amazing Christmas trip. This trip helped me to break-away from all of the sadness of my life. . .*When I got back to Miami, I had to go back to my messed-up life again.*

I remember making this small sculpture with my therapist, Janet. It had a sun, rainbow, and heart. The sun meant that it was going to be a better day, the rainbow meant to always be happy, and the heart was to love, no matter what. I gave it to this girl in my class, Whitney, but it was really meant for my mom. I often wonder where Whitney is today. She was very quiet.

My therapist, Ms. Janet, would have long conversations with me about my anger. She would give me strategies about how to deal with my anger.

CHAPTER 5

Glimpses of Law Enforcement and the Justice System

One day, Charlie Mae called me and told me that Wilson had been arrested. She had gotten together some money and wanted to go to his arraignment and see if she could make bail for him.

We went downtown to the courthouse and went into the courtroom. The district attorney and the public defender were standing up at the judge's bar. (The public defenders are widely referred to as "public pretenders.") There was a huge stack of records between them. A television screen came on, and there was a long line of people lined up in front of a camera at a jail which was remote from the courthouse. The first prisoner was asked his name, and the attorneys would try to find his record. Sometimes they could, and sometimes they couldn't. If they found it, they would review it and talk it over. It was obvious that they knew nothing about the cases beforehand. They would offer a plea right there, or bail, or occasionally hold without bail. The prisoner had about two minutes to accept or reject. When Wilson was next in line, they were able to find his record. They reviewed it, got together with the judge, and made him an offer. He took it and he was back home later that day.

It was not the first chance I had to observe the justice system as it relates to blacks and really all poor people. About five years before, a friend of mine who was a priest organized a retreat for persons with

AIDS. There were several who were quite ill, so my friend asked if I would attend in case anyone needed medical attention. I agreed to do so. While there, I noticed one lady who seemed very withdrawn. I went to speak with her. It turned out that her son had been in jail for almost six months. He had originally reported a neighbor for drug dealing. In retribution, that person accused him of threatening her with a gun. No gun was ever located, and his mother insisted there had never been one. Bail was $500,000, but these people were very poor, and they just couldn't come up with it. So there he sat for the last six months. I told her that as soon as the retreat was over, I would go down and bail him out. She was so relieved. That is exactly what we did. I think the charges were finally dropped, but he had lost six months of his life. Some of the statistics on the disparity of treatment between blacks and whites are appalling. Here is one study of individuals who were definitively exonerated by new DNA technology; in other words, it was later proved that they could NOT be guilty of the crime for which they were convicted. Many of them had eyewitness identification, some even had confessions (imagine how those were obtained). In this study over 60% of these proven wrongful convictions were black, in spite of blacks representing only about 12% of the population. The justice system is often cited as the great equalizer, the place where everyone can receive equal treatment, regardless of race. Really?

Then it became even more personal to me.

One night we had studied well so I took him to a local Gameworks afterward. I frequently did that as a reward. I dropeed Willie off at about 10:00p.m. at his house. As I left, I turned onto a road which bordered the predominantly black neighborhood where Willie lived, I was suddenly cut off on all sides by police cars, lights flashing, and a voice on the speaker saying get out of the car. I did as I was ordered, and they took me to the rear of my Lincoln and said, "Place your hands on the trunk." I did, while they proceeded to search the interior of my car. I asked why they had pulled me over. What had I done wrong?

They asked me what I was doing in that neighborhood. I replied that I tutored a kid and I had just gotten back from GameWorks and dropped him off. I said, "Here is the receipt," and reached for it in my pocket.

"Hands on the car!" they yelled as they drew a gun and pointed it directly at my head and cocked it. Now I was scared, but also angry.

"If you're looking for drugs, you're not going to find any," I said.

"What makes you think we are looking for drugs?" they said.

"I'm not stupid," I replied. After finding nothing, they said I could go. They were clearly disappointed that they had found nothing. They were not in the least apologetic that they had detained me for no reason and had actually held a loaded and cocked gun to my head. I asked the officer in charge if he had a moment. He said that he did. I asked him to take just a minute to go back to Willie's house and confirm my story. He said no. I looked over at another officer and asked, "What about you? Will you go with me?" I could see him receive a stare from the first officer. Then he also declined. I was still shaking by the time I reached home. I wanted to file a complaint but was afraid they would harass Willie's family in retribution if I did, so I dropped it. I always wondered why they stopped me THAT night, since I was in the neighborhood several nights a week. I also had so many confusing thoughts about that episode. What if they had chosen to plant some drugs? What if I had gone ahead and reached for the receipt and they had shot me? It was the first time I had personally been profiled and threatened. It gave a window to a whole new perspective. It has been said that the country was never more divided than on the day the O.J.'s verdict came down. Like the vast majority of whites, it had seemed like he was guilty to me. I couldn't really understand the point of view of the large majority of blacks. Now I could.

<u>DNA Exonerations in the United States</u>

Fast facts:

- **1989:** The first DNA exoneration took place
- **37:** States where exonerations have been won
- **20 of 351** people exonerated served time on death row
- **14:** Average length of time served by exonerees
- **4,788:** Total number of years served
- **26.5:** Average age of exonerees at the time of their wrongful conviction
- **42.5:** Average age at exoneration
- **38 of 351:** Pled guilty to crimes they did not commit
- **71%:** Involved eyewitness misidentification
  - 41% of these cases were a cross-racial misidentification
  - 32% of these cases involved multiple misidentifications of the same person
  - 27% of these cases involved misidentification through the use of a composite sketch
- **45%:** Involved misapplication of forensic science
- **28%:** Involved false confessions
  - 52% of the false confessors were 21 years old or younger at the time of arrest
  - 35% of the false confessors were 18 years old or younger at the time of arrest
  - 10% of the false confessors had mental health or mental capacity issues
- **17%:** Involved informants
- **256:** DNA exonerees compensated
- **183:** DNA exonerations worked on by the Innocence Project
- **150:** True suspects and/or perpetrators identified. Those actual perpetrators went on to be convicted of 147 additional violent crimes, including 77 sexual assaults, 35 murders, and 35 other violent crimes while the innocent sat behind bars for their earlier offenses.

<u>DNA Exonerations in the United States (cont'd)</u>

Races of the 351 exonerees:

217   African Americans

106   Caucasians

26   Latinos

2   Asian Americans

How DNA makes a difference in the criminal justice system

- Since 1989, there have been tens of thousands of cases where prime suspects were identified and pursued—until DNA testing (prior to conviction) proved that they were wrongly accused.
- In more than 25% of cases in a National Institute of Justice study, suspects were excluded once DNA testing was conducted during the criminal investigation (the study, conducted in 1995, included 10,060 cases where testing was performed by FBI labs).
- An Innocence Project review of our closed cases from 2004–June 2015 revealed that 29% of cases were closed because of lost or destroyed evidence.

Info Source: https://www.innocenceproject.org/dna-exonerations-in-the-united-states/

This was long before the Black Lives Matter Movement. Black lives certainly should matter. A lot of people were raised, like me, to believe that the police were good guys and on our side, there to protect us. Most probably still are. But that is often not the black experience. I understand both sides better now. I know that they were addressing huge pain, but I think that the founders of "Black Lives Matter" might have been better served to say "All Lives Matter—Equally!" Somehow, we must get past the division that has always existed between the races in this country and begin a HEALING process. In South Africa it was called reconciliation. Nelson Mandela was imprisoned for twenty-seven years. I can hardly imagine the grace it must have taken him not to be bitter. But he knew that "an eye for an eye leaves us all blind." So he forgave. The only condition was that the injustices had to be confessed. I wonder if we could pursue that here?

Donald Woods was a newspaper editor in South Africa in the 1970s. He became friends with Stephen Biko, a black activist who died while in police custody. Mr. Woods wrote a book about his experiences called BIKO and it was made into a movie, "Cry Freedom," with Kevin Klein as Donald Woods and Denzel Washington as Steven Biko. I met Mr. Woods at a book fair in Miami sometime in the 1980s. I pointed out to him that Mahatma Gandhi had actually begun his first non-violent protest in South Africa. He then took his concepts to India and freed that nation from British colonization. Dr. Martin Luther King Jr. then adopted those concepts into the civil rights movement in the United States. I asked Mr. Woods if he thought it might come full circle and be applied successfully in South Africa. He told me he didn't think that that would ever happen. In 1990 Nelson Mandela was released from prison. In 1994 he was elected the first Black President of South Africa and he oversaw the peaceful transition of that country from brutal apartheid to democracy.

Sometimes change takes longer than we would like. Sometimes it requires of us that we think bigger than we have ever thought before. Sometime it requires courage and even great sacrifice. Of course, Mahatma Gandhi and Dr. Martin Luther King Jr. both made the ultimate sacrifice when they were assassinated. But if we can keep faith, then the dream CAN be made manifest.

BLACK LIVES MATTER / ALL LIVES MATTER . . . The Struggle is REAL

I learned later in my life about an incident that happened to Mike after he left my house tutoring me one evening. I was told he was stopped by a South Miami police officer. He was questioned suspiciously and handcuffed. He kept telling him that he had just came back from a tutoring session. He offered to take them to my house to prove it. They didn't want to hear it. They suspected him of trying to buy drugs in the "BLACK" neighborhood. You see he always drove a large car – Lincoln Continental. They didn't realize that he was a medical doctor that was just trying to do something good for an inner- city boy. He experienced what Black men experience daily. He said he had never been so nervous and angry in his life. He had to learn how to deal with his anger and it wasn't easy. He never filed a complaint because he didn't want there to be any retaliation against me or my family, especially knowing the drug use history my family and neighborhood. WHY! ! !

CHAPTER 6

Willie began junior high. He was away from the direct influence of the counselor, whom I had worked so closely with. I was also less familiar with the new teacher and staff. They treated [him] more like an average student, which one could argue he should have been ready for after over four years of extensive efforts by me and the program he had been in. Sometimes, things just develop an inertia of their own and it takes awareness and effort to avoid stagnation. But for whatever reasons, he was still not ready. His decline was gradual, not precipitous. He would still do well in most classes, but then he would foul up, largely for lack of effort. The same thing applied to my work with Willie; his active participation waned. I was putting more and more effort in for less and less result.

One of the things that continued to be a bond was basketball.

I was at the Community Center one day, waiting for Willie to finish playing basketball. Standing outside I noticed two boys about five or six years old, with their faces pressed up against the glass to the window, looking in. I walked outside and asked them why they didn't come inside and play. They responded that they didn't have any shoes, which were required for you to enter. As soon as Willie was finished, the four of us went to find their mother to get permission to buy those shoes. When we got to the apartment, it turned out that there were three families all living in one apartment, totaling fifteen kids all under the age of eighteen. They ALL needed shoes! I had Willie take down each person's name and shoe size, and the two of us went to the shoes store to buy them shoes. Nothing designer, just regular sneakers. We returned to the apartment, and within minutes, everyone had their new shoes on and were off to play. I don't remember anyone, child or parent, saying thank you. It is said that if an act of kindness is performed with the expectation of receiving thanks, then it is not really an act of kindness but a transaction.

Many, many episodes occurred over those next few years. Some of the stories are worth telling because they have lessons within themselves. One such story involved a friend of Willie's dad. One night, I got a call at home after I got home after a tutoring session. "Doc, is that you?" a man asked. I had never really liked being called "doc," but in that community that was how I had become known.

"Yes, it's me. Who is this?" I asked.

He told me who he was and that he had seen two young guys trying to use my credit cards. He actually confronted them and took back my wallet and cards, which apparently had dropped out of my car when I left Willie's earlier. I thanked him and arranged to meet him the next day. I met him and he returned everything intact. He never asked for anything in return. About two years later, he ran into me outside of Willie's house. Unknown to me had an eight-month-old child. He told me that lately he felt as if he couldn't hold the baby like before. I briefly did some muscle testing on him, and it did seem like there was a subtle weakness in certain muscles. I told him to go to the ER and I would arrange to have him seen by a specialist. He had no health insurance. I called the ER and told them to register him as a patient and place a consult with the on-call specialist. When I checked in that evening, I was told that he arrived and registered as I directed. The consultant was notified. The patient waited almost six hours. Then the consultant came, loudly asked, "Where is this charity patient I am supposed to see?" He was directed to the patient, did a very brief exam, and declared he didn't find anything wrong with him and discharged him. I do not believe that I ever saw the patient again. About six months later, he was admitted to another hospital where they found a tumor wrapped around his spinal cord. He died during that admission. He probably would have had no different result if we had found it at the earlier visit. But he certainly deserved to be treated with more dignity and respect. It made me sad.

Middle School memories

I left Ludlum Elementary school after the 5ᵗʰ Grade. I went to a school called Ruth Owens Kruse. It was a lot like TOPS but bigger and lots of students. Kruse was a school for students with emotional and behavioral problems. I would ride the school bus every day with people I knew and eventually people I got to know.

I remember every morning before I would get on the bus I would always have breakfast. My Mom made sure I ate, every day. She would cook my favorite bacon, eggs, and grits. If not, I would call Mike and we would be to Krispy Kreme or McDonalds, his favorite.

When I got to Middle School, I wasn't nearly as shy I was used to be. I met a girl that became my first girlfriend. Her name was Ayana Jones. She had a great personality and she was very confident. I liked her a lot because she wasn't afraid to approach me. She just came right up to me and let me know that she was interested in me. Wow! You know, however, she never got a chance to meet my mom. I wasn't sure she could handle what my Mom was all about with the drugs and the way she looked with that burn on her neck. We kept out relationship at school. I was with her from my sixth grade to my seventh -grade year. One good thing about us was we never had sex. I wasn't ready for that yet.

One time while I was at Kruse we had a talent show. I was so cool. I was a model and had to walk down the runway at school. I was dressed in all white -Levi's, white bling Kool-Aid t-shirt. I got over being shy or nervous that night.

In my Art class we made these wooden race cars. You see you had to make them a certain way so that they would be fast. Of course, you know I had one of the top five fastest cars. The cars were small and they looked like little Nascars. They had CO2's in the back. We would line our cars up and race each other.

I passed Math with flying colors. Math was always my favorite subject. I loved all kinds of math. I related it to life. We all need math to survive.

I learned how to wrestle in P.E. I got my first matchup against a kid whose name is John. I beat him quick in front of the class. He didn't' like the fact that he lost. So, he got big headed and wanted to fight me. He threw a crazy punch at me and I ducked it. I, then, picked him up and dropped him hard on the ground. That was the only fight I ever had in Middle School.

In my eighth- grade year. I was really starting to enjoy school on my own without much help. I was placed in Woodshop and outdoor activities. We went on a fieldtrip to the jail house. I didn't like it in there. I didn't like not having my freedom. That was scary.

It was at the end of this year that my whole world was turned upside down...

CHAPTER 7

Money

Slowly, almost insidiously, it began to creep in. Money. The first was the phone as I mentioned before. That was my idea and was more for my convenience. The next was the laundry. The house was filled with dirty laundry. I had no way of knowing what clothes Willie actually had and what he might need. So one day I said to Charlie Mae, "Why don't you and your daughters gather up all of the laundry? I'll take you over to the laundromat, and you can spend a whole day and get caught up." She was fine with the idea. Charlie Mae was not averse to work, as long as she was clearly directed and she was not high. So they gathered it all up and put it in my trunk. It was a large trunk but we couldn't even close it. We drove to the laundromat and unloaded. That whole day they washed, dried, and folded. I paid for the washers and dryers. That was the first time. After that, about once a month, she would ask to go again. It kind of became a humorous thing. I think the max was thirty loads. Indeed, they were all their clothes. Thirty loads to wash and dry cost me about fifty dollars. That was still so little to me, and they were all doing the work. Then one day, as I was getting in my car to leave from a tutoring session, Charlie Mae said the rent man was coming and she was a hundred dollars short. She asked if I could help her out a little. I was taken unprepared. It seemed so little to me and I said yes. It became a monthly thing. You can call me a sucker, an enabler—trying to buy their favor, assuaging white guilt. There may be some truth to all of those, but at the bottom of it all is that, sadly, the amounts that kept them from being evicted were so small to me that I hardly noticed. I was so focused on trying to achieve a positive outcome for Willie. As long as he was progressing, a couple hundred a month didn't concern me.

Finally, I knew I should confront the situation with Charlie Mae and money. I told her I wouldn't be continuing to help her out with the rent. I thought surely she would get a small job to make some money, or that she would ask me for it anyway. Neither one. She wasn't the least bit angry with me. But within a few months, they were evicted. Had to move into one room of a house, all five of them, sharing one bathroom and one kitchen with two other families.

I don't recall exactly how long they stayed in those circumstances—maybe a year, year and a half. It didn't seem to bother the rest of his family. But I could tell it was bothering Willie. His grades began slipping further; absences from school began to increase. I just couldn't stand seeing him in that mess. It was eroding much of the progress we had achieved. So, I made Charlie Mae an offer: I would rent a two-bedroom apartment for them and pay for it as long as she met two conditions: First, she had to stop using drugs. Second, she could not allow Wilson to live there. The drugs and the abuse were just too toxic for me to allow. Maybe it was unrealistic. However, she had completely quit when she was pregnant with Willie, so I knew that she could do it. Maybe I was interfering in her life way too much. Anyway, she agreed. I got them an apartment. She seemed to be dong alight. I visited there one day and there were multiple electrical cords stringing out of the apartment. Apparently, some of her neighbors had their electricity cut off, and she was supplying them with electricity at my expense. Honestly, I never found out for sure if she was charging them or just doing it out of the kindness of her heart. I was pretty sure that she was back to using, and there was evidence that Wilson was back. I was going to talk with her about everything as soon as I had the time. But as Shakespeare has Julius Caesar say, "Time and tide wait for no man."

CHAPTER 8

Charlie Mae Death

I had just seen Charlie Mae that morning, walking along the side-walk, looking happy as she waved to me. Late that afternoon I got a call from one of my ER doctors, all of whom knew Willie and most of his family by now. "You better come in," she said. I got there quickly. Charlie Mae was already completely unresponsive and on a mechanical ventilator. She had a CT of the brain, which showed a large bleed. She had done too much cocaine. It was very unlikely she would survive. I left to go find Willie. First, I found his sister, Leslie. I explained the situation to her. She started crying. I told her that we needed to find Willie. She calmed down enough to go search for him. She found him, and I told him the situation as well. He showed almost no emotion. I said that they needed to come with me to the hospital. He didn't want to go. I told him this would likely be the last time for him to see her and say goodbye. I insisted that he come with me. He did so reluctantly. We went in to the room where she was. Leslie started to cry again. Willie was still emotionless. I took Charlie Mae's hand in mine and started talking to her. I told her that Leslie and Willie were there with me. Leslie went over and put her head down on her mother, still sobbing. The ER nurses and doctor were very kind. They attempted to comfort Leslie. Willie kept at a distance.

After a time, I suggested we go. We went to the apartment where people were beginning to congregate. I explained to them the situation and that I doubted that she would survive the night. I went home. I got the call in the middle of the night that she had passed.

The next morning, I went over to the apartment. Arrangements were being made by Charlie Mae's family over at his grandmother's house. Wilson was alone in the apartment. It was probably the only time we had ever talked alone. I asked him why he had never been more supportive of Willie and my efforts. First he said that he wasn't ever sure Willie was his son. I pointed out to him that he had raised him like he was, lived in the same house, and whether he actually was his father or not, why did he always run Willie down, call him fat and stupid, rather than trying to encourage him and build him up? Neither one of us were mad or even raising our voices. I was honestly trying to understand. It was such a totally different reality than I had grown up with. Finally, he said, "Doc, we are like crabs in a bucket." Having grown up on the Gulf Coast and been crabbing many times in my youth, I could picture exactly what he was saying. When you have a bunch of crabs in a bucket, they will crawl all over each other, trying to get out. But as soon as one gets anywhere near the top of the bucket, one below grabs him and tries to pull itself up and they all fall down. I was speechless. There was really nothing left to say. I went over to Willie's grandmother's house. They said the funeral director needed $1000 more and could I help out. I said that I would and asked for his number. They said to just give them the cash and they would take care of it. I said I needed to talk to him. They didn't want to give me his number. Finally, I went outside, found out where she was going to be buried, and called them. The funeral home didn't know anything about needing more money. I left. I realized that nobody had seen Willie. I drove around a little and finally found him shooting baskets at the park. I watched him from a distance for a while. He was totally absorbed in what he was doing. I drove him home with many sad and conflicting thoughts.

The funeral was in a few days. The church was filled. Me and my partner arrived as the service was beginning. We were the only white people there. We went in, probably looking a little lost. Some ladies dressed all in white saw us and seated us. I don't remember that much about the service except that the immediate family, including Willie, were all seated down in the front row. All except Wilson, who was absent. Once the church service was over, everybody filed out, going by the open casket and the family. Willie barely even looked up. We got in our car and followed to the cemetery. There we parked and walked to the gravesite. I finally saw Wilson way off by himself. He had been totally ostracized the entire time. Back at Willie's grandmother's house, there was a reception. I spoke briefly with his grandmother. "He killed her," she said, referring to Wilson. "All of those years of beatings and drugs killed her. I should have killed him a long time ago." Again, Willie was nowhere to be found. Weeks later we were together, and he asked me, "Do you know why I didn't cry when my mother died?" I asked why. "Because I knew she wasn't getting beaten up anymore."

The apartment couldn't be occupied by just minors, so the kids all went to live with various relatives. Willie went to live with an aunt. The school year was just about over. Willie was now going into high school. The loss of his mother was devastating to him. He had always both idolized her and idealized her. He never really processed how much she had contributed to her own downfall and eventual death. Nor to his problems. As far as I know, he never did cry about her.

My mother died at the end of my 8th grade. I struggled to finish that year. I lost my pride and joy when she died. I went into a shell. I began to disconnect from Mike and the family. I was lost. I stopped talking to my Dad. I blamed him for her death. I felt it was his fault that my Mom died. All those beatings, hits upside her head along with the drugs just took her out.

The funeral was such a blur for me. I sat next to my sister. Everyone looking at us. I could hear the crying, screaming and singing. My Grandma was so sad. You're not supposed to bury your child. So many people and I didn't want to be there. I felt like a tadpole in the middle of the ocean. I just didn't want to have to talk to anybody. What I hated most of all was having to go to the gravesite – Paradise – down in Richmond Heights. I was going to have to leave my Mom there. Cars lined up the pathway to her final resting place.

My heart was so broken. How could this be happening to me? What was I going to do?

My Dad standing around away from the family because he knew they hated him. They were telling everyone it was his fault. He tried to distance himself from the family. My oldest sister was incarcerated but was able to attend the funeral with supervision.

An Ordinary Day . . . Final Farewell to Mom, My Rock!

This day, May 6th, started off as any other day. I didn't know it would be the last day my mom would live on this Earth.

Early evening on May 6th, I asked my Mom if I could go spend the night at my cousin's house. I just wanted to go hang out and have fun. She told me ok and I packed my clothes and off I went. It was just an ordinary day. We just wanted to have fun hanging out being teenagers.

I immediately left home. I got there and immediately started to play video games. Later on, that evening as we were sitting around kicking it and watching TV, there was a knock on the door. It was around 11:00 pm. The knock was Mike. I was startled to see him at that hour. "What's up Mike?" I asked. He slowly began to tell me that my Mom had a stroke and it didn't look good. He said he'd gotten a call from South Miami Hospital and they wanted him bring my sister and me right away. Of course, they would call Mike. He worked there and everyone knew about his long-standing relationship with our family. A million thoughts ran across my mind. I couldn't believe the words that were coming out of his mouth. "WHAT!!!", "Oh my God . . . this couldn't be true!!!"

As I gathered my thoughts we quickly took off to the hospital but we had to go get my baby sister, Leslie. We picked her up and Mike began to tell her the awful news. She began to cry hysterically. I couldn't cry. I was in shock.

As we approached the hospital, Mike parked the car and off we went to find my Mom. As we approached her room, we found her covered with tubes coming in & out of her body with the ventilator breathing for her. The room was quiet except for the hissing sounds of the machine that kept her alive long enough for us to say our goodbyes.

Mike encouraged us to talk to her because even though she was unconscientious, she could still hear. I quietly bent down by her ear and softly said. . . "Mom, I'm here for you. I love you. I will always be here for you." I repeated it several times to her. My sister was sobbing uncontrollably, shocked by the reality and I just looked at her in silence. I knew in my head that technically she was dead and they were simply keeping her on the machine until we got there.

After we said our goodbyes It was finally time to leave. Our final visit came to a dreadful end. My sister and I decided to walk home. I remember the streets were consumed in darkness. We didn't want Mike to drive us. We just wanted to walk and be alone. As we exited the hospital, I punched a window out of a car in anger. I was so angry I didn't care. My tears began to flow with the reality of knowing my Mom was gone for good. My sister and I just slowly walked back to the "Townhouses" with tears flowing from our eyes. I needed to clear my head and think. "***Our rock, our everything*** was gone..." How am I suppose to live through this? How am I suppose to move forward? **God Help Me!**

CHAPTER 9

On His Own

After the death of his mother, Willie seemed to change. Where getting him motivated was difficult, now it seemed it was almost impossible to maintain any effort. In retrospect, I was still trying to work with my paradigm, not his. I enrolled him in the public high school near me. It was, of course, predominantly white. The students were mostly in stable homes and well on their way to college. I am sure he felt out of place and intimidated. It also required a commute from his aunt's. I bought him a pass on the public transportation. While others have overcome such obstacles and worse, Willie still lacked the self-motivation to do it. He didn't last long there; he basically withdrew himself and registered into a high school near him which was nearly all black. I saw it occasionally, and to me it almost looked like a prison. It was surrounded by a tall, chain-link fence with barbwire on top. He found a teacher that seemed to take interest in him, but Willie just couldn't seem to finish anything. He failed several classes and came back next year with the same problems and eventually dropped out. He would keep in touch with me periodically. He informed me about his sisters; one was in and out of an abusive relationship.

One day she got beaten badly and staggered, bleeding, to the bus stop to get to the hospital. The bus driver called 911. When EMS and police arrived, they determined she was in violation of parole and took her to jail on the spot. During this time, Willie had told me that if he just had a stable place, he could hold down a job and support himself. I got him an apartment in the neighborhood where he grew up. I paid first, and last deposit, furnished it, and got the electricity turned on. I went over a very basic budget with him. He could have made enough to keep an apartment with a minimum wage job. I don't think he ever got a job. If he did, he didn't keep it. He got evicted and started talking about Georgia, and his plans of maybe moving there, considering he had some family residing there at time. I thought the change in location may be for the best, especially since it was a small town and he knew some people. I eventually bought him a bus ticket and took him to the bus station and off he went. He would occasionally call, but it was hard for me to tell how he was actually doing. He actually wrote to me several times. He began talking more and more about God. This brought my mind something that had occurred way back when Willie was in elementary school. He had an assignment to write about a Bible story. Upon questioning, I was surprised to find that he knew nothing about the Bible. I knew that he had gone to Sunday school. I didn't know if he had just gone and didn't pay any attention or what. I chose the story of David and the Goliath. I had not read it in a long time.

Why this episode occurred to me after all of these years, I am not sure. Maybe the significance is that in it David says to Goliath: "Thou comest with a sword, and with a spear, and with a shield, but I come with the name of the Lord . . . The Lord saveth not with a sword and spear, for the battle is the Lord's and he will deliver into our hands" (Sam. 17:46).

As I reflect on this now, I feel like what is saying to me is that this is not a struggle of just the physical world, of money and budgets and work ethic and material things. Focusing on those may appear to bring about some results but they are temporal and will fade away. In Willie's life, and ultimately in all of our lives, if we want to achieve lasting change and have enduring peace, the work must be done on a spiritual level.

After nine or ten months, he was bored, couldn't find work, and was saying the people he was staying with didn't really want him there. He eventually returned to Miami. Someone had told me that he was wanted by the police. I went and found him and convinced him to turn himself in. I went with him to the police station where he identified himself, they took him to the back, and wouldn't tell me anything. Not what he was charged with, where he would be located, or where he would be arraigned. Nothing. I finally left and later learned that he was charged with attempting to distribute drugs and he was never convicted. Sometime later, his sister called me crying and said that Willie had been shot in the back and was in the OR in the trauma center. I went there and he had indeed been shot in the back. He had one lung collapsed and the bullet was lodged just behind his heart. Nevertheless, he was discharged within about three days. They never confirmed if he had any place to go. This time I took him home and he recovered there. He wanted to return to Georgia so I put him on the bus once again.

There were multiple witnesses to the actual shooting. Everyone knew who had shot Willie and that Willie was unarmed. In spite of that, no arrest was ever made.

In high school I learned to be a gentleman and that I couldn't do whatever I wanted to do. One person that I could talk to about anything was Mike. Mike was like family to me. Things began to get rough so I started smoking black and mild's and weed to clear my head. I was trying to make sense of my confused world. I was suddenly thrust into manhood without prior training.

I left Palmetto Senior High and started attending Miami Northwestern Senior High where I had to sign up as homeless. I was staying with my aunt Linda. When I came to the city, I was tried to make friends but the guys on the street begin to try me. They must have thought I was "soft." I had to arm myself with a gun for safety. I started becoming real familiar with all kinds of guns. This was my new world and I had to protect myself.

One day I was with my friend, Elijah, in South Miami. While hanging out with him he told these guys had a beef with him. As we were walking I gave him my last $4 and told him to go home in the city. It was too dangerous until things cooled down. As we were talking the guys approached him and they got into a fight. I stood there frozen in disbelief. I yelled out, ... "I am not going to just watch yawl hurt my friend - Hell no." They were armed with knives, guns and bats. I couldn't let them hurt my friend. I would have to go down with him. He was my friend. He ran to get away and they began chasing him with knives and bats. Suddenly they stopped chasing him and came back to jump on me. He was able to get away to get home with the last four dollars I gave him. When they came back they threatened me. I had my gun and told them to get away from me. They left but I knew it wasn't over.

Later on, that night, I was just chillin' in the projects and I saw two cars circling. I felt like it retaliation . . . it was for me. It was about 10:00 pm and it was a school night. My sister came with my nephew to take me home. I told her to go home and I should be home in thirty minutes. They were looking for my friend. He was already gone home. I was with my homeboys, Van and Jeff. We started walking through the project. The guys jumped out the car with two machetes, shotguns and a pistol. As they approached my friends they questioned them about their involvement in the earlier incident. They answered "NO." They begin to circle me. They tried to pistol whip me but I ducked the strokes and body slammed two of them. I took off and I got cut by the machete and as I was running. They fired the first shot that missed me but the second on hit me in my back near my heart and one in the ankle. I ran across the street and I fell. I became unconscious. When I tried to get up I could still hear bullets being fired. They tried to fire more bullets into me they must have ran out of bullets. All I heard were the clicks of an empty gun. I later heard more shots but I think it must have been my homeboys firing at them. I was air- lifted to Jackson Memorial Hospital. I was in critical condition and had to be resuscitated. I was close to dying. While in the hospital, I was in bad shape. The recovery was tough. What was I going to do now? Where will I go?

Mike was contacted and he immediately came to see about me. I'm sure he couldn't believe his eyes. In his mind I'm sure he asked, "What the hell has Willie gotten himself into?"

When I left the hospital, I stayed with Mike for about two weeks. I stayed there so I could get my head together and for safety. I needed to try and figure out what I needed to do next. After all, I was homeless. I couldn't deal with the drama and stress.

Mike encouraged me to go back to school. So, I did for one day. When I got there my counselor questioned me about my absences. I told them I had been shot. They wanted to know why the school wasn't notified. Why didn't I call for an exception? I just couldn't deal with the harsh scrutiny they were giving me. They didn't understand that I told no one. I couldn't.

I crawled back in my shell and never returned to school again. I became a *dropout*. Mike was not happy and encouraged me to go live with some of my Mom's friends. I did that for a while and got tired and began house surfing again.

After being by myself with no place to go, I began selling drugs. I was already familiar with that world – especially in South Miami. I had disconnected from Mike. Our monthly Social Security dependents check was cut off and I had to fin for myself. I was tired of asking for handouts. I was exposed to the drug world very early. I innocently started really around now the age of 9 or 10 years old. The dope boys would ask me to take packages to people and they would give me money. Later, I would become a look out for the dope boys in the neighborhood – "Nines coming down" was the code word. My mom was alive. My dad was there. But now I'm doing it. I knew better but I had to survive. I had to serve. I had to eat. I knew it was wrong. I served. I was giving them the same thing that helped killed my Mom. I was selling drugs to my own kind. I had to do something to feed myself but I was just as guilty as all the rest. Here I was selling this poison to my own people – killing them. Then, I started serving myself– smoking my own products. I was so messed up. The bad thing about it was I was smoking up all my profits.

With drug dealing you have to protect yourself. I had to carry guns for my protection. I took them to school – nines, forties, Glocks, 38's. All types. I was always armed. Having to live in the Pork-N-Beans you better be armed. Everyone is trying to protect their territories. No one is loyal.

I began to skip school but my school grades were good enough for me to play sports for the school. It was hard because I didn't want to play without my number one fan. Every day I think about my mother and what my life would have been like if I didn't have her for the fifteen years I did. I felt as if I needed and wanted to be where she is but I had to be strong for my two big sisters.

One evening the South Miami Police did a big drug sweep. We were all arrested. I got arrested for selling drugs. There was a news flash on TV of a South Miami drug sweep and my face was one of the 30 arrested that evening – 24 resulted in no charges. It was a bogus charge. I hung around drug dealers but they had no proof or outstanding charges on me. I never served time for that ... BOGUS!

One night I was in my friend's room across from mine and suddenly I hear "BAMMMM". My door has been kicked in by the Police. I ran and hid for 3 hours as they raided my room looking for drugs. After they left, I called Mike. We talked about the situation. He told me the best thing I should do was to surrender. The next day Mike took me so that I could turn myself in. I was immediately released because they had to outstanding warrants on me.

I was used to being held up by Police in Liberty City, especially on Tuesday and Thursdays. We would just be sitting on the street and cops would come by and we had to lay flat with hands behind our backs, shoes and socks off, pictures of tattoos taken. All because we were sitting on the streets / BLACK. – not bothering anyone. WHY?

I went to Georgia to be with my cousins for about 2 years. I needed to get away after being shot and living in fear of my life. I needed to separate from the lifestyle I was accustom to living in the streets.

My cousins agreed to let me come and stay with them for a while. They were struggling financially but they loved and helped each other. They would sit and eat together every day. They would go to church every Sunday. I was use to going to church. As a young-ster – church every Sunday was not big deal. In our neighborhood Church was where we had to go no matter what. I would go and see my friends from school and the neighborhood. My mom would make me go but I had never experienced that kind of togetherness this family had.

While in Georgia, I met a very special lady. She had 3 kids that I grew to love. As the relationship progressed I would take care of them while she was at work. I was at peace, at least I thought I was . . . long story short. It didn't work out. I knew it was too good to be true. After an altercation with her ex, I had to end the relationship. He was accusing me of mistreating her. During this time, I carried a gun for safety. I didn't need a confrontation that could become a deadly one so we just called it quits. Heartbroken, I eventually returned to Miami, putting the guns down for good.

As you read this book I would like you know and understand that I have had a life that many would only envy. Having a mentor, like Mike, to provide me with so many opportunities and yet I still struggle. I never thought I was worth it. Mike sacrificed so much for me. He donated his time and his money in trying to make me a better person. He's loved me through all my mess and pain. He's turned me in and got me out of jail. Most people would envy out relationship. I guess it's true that you can take a person out of the Ghetto but you can't take the Ghetto out of them. That would be me. I still struggle with that mentality. I can't seem to get out of my own way.

Life without Mike – I don't know. Nobody in the streets cared for me like him. I probably would be locked up or would have killed my Dad because he was so abusive to my Mom. Who knows? I pray and thank God for Mike in my life every day.

You have to cherish what is given to you... YOU can't take it for granted. If you have a Coach, Mentor, or teacher tell them what you're going through. They're your father's or mother's when you're not at home. Be honest - it's in your best interest.

Here I am today still trying to find my purpose in life. I am still surfing from house to house of family members and friends. I still find myself involved in family struggles, oftentimes, finding myself in dangerous situations. Now that I'm a man, it's very hard for me to sit back and witness domestic violence so I have been sent on my way when I voice my opinion. I am working now. I'm trying to save up enough money to afford my own place one day. I know there's a light at the end of the tunnel. I still trying to find it!

CHAPTER 10

Return, Betrayal

In 2015, I received a letter from Willie:

Dear: Mike

This has been the haldest 8 years of my life. I haven't visit my mom in eight whole years and it's been killing me in my inside. But scent I found God in my life I been humble and hungry to go back to school. I'm ready to come back home but all I need is a place to call home not just somewhere to stay. If I can stay with you I promise I will do right caused god blessed me with you in my life. He could of gave you anybody in this world but he picked me for you and you for me. I thank him everyday for putting you and dean in my life. If it wasn't for you I would been in jail or in a grave by now but God sent me to Georgia so I can get close to him why I'm up here but I will be doing the something when I find a stayable place. I found myself up here cause I see how real and hald life can be without dreams or Goals. But you is the only one that was always there for me even though the good things and the bad things I did. I'm greatful for everything you did for me and my friends. I told you I was going to write you back so I'm going to keep my word now on. I'm tired of feeling like a nobody. When I am somebody that is smart, helpful, and greatful. I now see I can't make it on my own caused you always going to need help, or somebody to pick you up when a person is down. Here I am telling you I need you in my life to keep me on the right road you and my family is the only one's that makes me want to live, but if I lose you like I lose my family at once in my life I will lose my mind. I need your help with catching up with reading and school. I sorry if I every said or did anything to hurt you when I was young or now. Mike I appreciate you with all my heart and I mean that from the bottom of my heart. I asking you for one big favorite right now I want you to help me get my life back on track. So I can be the man my mom wanted me to be. I promise you I'm going to give you 200 percents out of me. When I say 200 percents I'm talking about in them books every-day and I'm going to go to church every Sunday, pride and not overclasses,

All I want is a place where its peace
and quiet so I can handle my business. Mike
I love you like you my dad and I respect you to the fullest. I look up to you
cause you is a great, and awsome femodel for me
I just can't be around the wrong people. I
stopped smoking weed cause it don't fix my
problems. So will you give me a second chance or any more chance to get on track. I
been sleep in a car for like 3 months caused
I don't want nobody thinking I'm useing them.
But I'm just thankful just to see another
day because somebody didn't wake up this
morning and it could of been me or you but I'm
thankful he keeping you around for me. I won't
know what to do if I lose you without
making you pride of me why you living because I can make
my mom pride in seiritaul. I pray myself to
sleep mostly every night caused to devil been
trying to attack me in all types of ways but
god got me in his hands and I'm not
running away from him no where not in Georgia or not in Miami. The best thing for
me is to live with you I promise you won't
know I'm their.
PS. Willie Bentley I love you Mike like a daddy

It seemed sincere. It touched my heart. I got him a bus ticket back from Georgia. One of Willie's friends seemed to have been on the right path. The friend had actually been away at college for two years supporting himself. Now the friend found himself in difficult times. He was living out of his car, but at least he had a car. Willie had never obtained his driver's license. So, in my way of thinking, this could be a win-win situation. I could help both of them find an apartment, which I did. Both had bad credit, so the only do it was to pay six month's rent in advance, which I did. I asked them to pay me back over those six months, which they easily could have done with low-paying jobs. The friend could help Willie with transportation, and it could work out for everybody—in my world. In their world, they started arguing about everything. Willie might have paid me one month, his friend for two, but there was no real effort, no mutual support. I was going out of town for a week, and I asked Willie if he could watch my house. I told Willie he could stay there, if he wanted to, but that NOBODY else could. If he felt bored or lonely, he could always go back to his apartment. I explained to him the concepts of liability, etc. and he understood. When I got back to the house, it looked in good order. Nothing was missing and it appeared clean. Then I learned that he had breached my trust and had a party there. Furthermore, he had actually driven my vehicles. He had no driver's license or insurance.

I felt totally betrayed. I told him that I could not help him anymore. I did say that I still cared about him, and wished him only the best. It was a very sad time for me. He called me some months later. He had apologized at the time and several times afterward. Another time he had called to apologize, he actually had a quite interesting suggestion. He wanted to write a book about the experiences we had shared. What an irony! The person I had hoped to teach to read now wanted to write a book. Of course, he knew nothing about how to go about writing a book, and neither did I. After some thought, I suggested to him that we each write about our experiences. I would write and describe from my perspective, and he would do the same from his perspective and in his own words the experiences we had shared over the years. Then we would put them side-by-side and publish it. That is what we present here. Views of the same experiences, but from perspectives and backgrounds that could not be more different. We were literally polar opposites. One white, one black. One relatively wealthy, one penniless. One from a stable loving home where there was no violence or drugs, where I was totally supported and told that all things were possible. The other, from a home where violence was an everyday occurrence. Where drugs and alcohol regularly placed people in an altered state of mind. One where he was constantly told he was stupid, that he would never make it. These differences are so profound, so deep, that there are almost too much to bridge. But bridge them we must, for in the end we really are all one, and so this divide exists within us, and will surely destroy us if we do not heal it.

I doubt that this country is at the point where it attempts such an effort. Everyone is so busy just trying to get by, and so totally convinced that theirs is the "right way." If the country is not ready, then maybe one state, or even one neighborhood, one school . . . Who knows?

But even if none of those are ready, do not use that as an excuse and give up. Go inside yourself. It may not be easy. Others may not support or understand you. But as Mahatma Ghandi said, "You must be the change you wish to see in this world".

Then, once you are deep inside yourself, paradoxically you must lose your "self," get completely outside of your "self" and totally enter into larger reality. Then come back to yourself with new knowledge, with a new vision. Transformed, even transcendent.

> We shall not cease from exploration and the end of
> all our exploring will be to arrive where we began
> and to know the place for the first time.
>
> —T. S. Elliot

- **Trust & The Betrayal . . . The Trip**
- I owe Mike so much. I could never repay him. He tries to believe in me but I have disappointed him so many times I had come back to Miami after living in Georgia.
- A few years ago, Mike got me my first apartment in South Miami. I had been going from one house to another – friends and family. Mike decided to rent it for me to help me get on my feet. The apartment was Sunset Place, right across the street from South Miami Hospital. When I was younger I remember my friends and I would sneak in this apartment complex to swim in the pool and to think that I now had an apartment in this place. It had one bedroom with two closets, AC, balcony but no central air-condition-ing. It was really a very nice place. My cousin was my room-mate. We lived together for eight months. The agreement was that I would go back to school and get a job. I was going but I would later find out my cousin was telling Mike things behind my back. He was jealous of our relationship. The last thing he told Mike shook our relationship but I had to take responsibility for my actions. I felt like Keyon was doing this to sabotage my relationship with Mike and he would help him more. This is what happen . . .
- Mike was preparing to travel for a week. In preparation for his trip he offered his home to me. He explained that I could come over and chill if I needed to. He sat at the table with me and explained how important it was for him to trust me. He explained about the liability and insur-ances of the house and car. I was to be there alone and not drive his car. He discussed the consequences if I didn't follow his instructions.
- After Mike left for his trip, I did go over to his house. It is a big house so I invited a female to come over and spend the night with me. I was afraid of being there alone. I borrowed his car. I rode around town. Later, a few other friends came over – maybe eight-. I was enjoying this gath-ering. I had never been able to have fun like that. They got

in the pool and we had some music on. Nothing in the house was broken or stolen. There were no drugs. However, one of Mike's back lights on his car got busted out. OMG. I was just enjoying the moment. I threw caution to the wind. I totally wasn't thinking. I was showing off to my friends. I knew there were consequences. This was the first time I had ever done anything like this. I should have confessed to Mike when he got back but I didn't. I was waiting on the right time.

- When Mike got back home, my cousin, Keyon, called and told Mike everything. You see, he and I had a big quarrel. How could he do that to me. He just wanted to get into Mikes good graces. I'm the one that talked Mike into getting him a job at South Miami Hospital. I'm the one that would ask Mike to help him along with me. Yes, he was doing what was expected. He was going to school and working. I felt like he was becoming more favored than me.

- After Mike got the news, he immediately questioned me. I couldn't lie. I felt so betrayed by Keyon and Mike felt betrayed by me. I disappointed Mike like no other time before. He could have lost everything due to my stupidity. I lacked respect for his property. Our relationship of trust was severed because I was simply too selfish. He would never trust me again. How could I have done this to the one person in the world that cared so much for me. I apologized wholeheartedly. I know I hurt him badly. Will Mike ever trust me again?

- . . . I doubt it!

Dedications to Mike & Mom!

Mike,

I appreciate everything you have done for me. You helped me to become a better man despite my circumstances and our differences. You showed me love as a Big Brother and as a Father. You showed me how I needed to work for what I wanted. You gave me the tough love when needed to steer me in the right direction. Things I would have never known as a man today.

One regret I have is that I was unable to be at your parent's funerals. I know that we were going through a tough time. I just wish I could have been there for you as you were there for me when my Mom died.

Remember, what I have become is not your fault. You tried to do everything in your power to steer me right. My mom asked you to watch over me and you have certainly done that. I will continue to try and make you proud of me.

When I got shot, it took so much out of me. It was as though I gave up. I stopped going to school. Lost interest in trying to achieve my goals. All the things you fought so hard for me to achieve.

I will always love you as much as you loved me. Money isn't everything! I truly appreciate you. You showed me enough to survive. I hope you never feel that I used you. I'm truly sorry for the many disappointments. I strayed from my goals. The best is yet to come. I endured a lot of bumps in the road but I'm not done yet . . . just wait and see! God's not through with me yet... you've been my Guardian Angel through it all.

Willie

Dear Mom,

Mom you were my best friend. I saw the pain that you went through. I loved you so much for doing everything possible to help me have a better life than you. I thank you for showing me how to treat a woman and for teaching me how to have manners. Even though we were poor you kept a roof over my head, food in my mouth, and your unconditional love. You showed me how to survive during the tough times. You made sure to teach me how to cook even if it's just your favorite meal every day. You had one of the kindest hearts for a person who went through so much and kept a smile on your face. You made me go to church with grandma every Sunday. You used to feed people who were hungry, especially the crack heads and homeless people when there was extra to give away. You were never shy about doing it. You loved to play sports like track, softball, and shooting pool. I miss holding you at night to make you feel safe and keeping you humble even when you just got beat on. I watched you have a bloody nose and two black eyes when I was in the same house. I remember you telling me to promise to never put my hands on a woman. I remember you teaching me how to ride a bike. You came to all my football, basketball, soccer, and baseball games. You were such a proud mother for what you had raised me to be. I remember when kids used to disrespect you in front of me by cracking jokes on you which caused me to get in a lot of fights. If it was about you mom I would have gone to the grave with you. I have been staying with friends and family to get back on my feet - which is nothing like living with you mom. You gave me a bookbag full of school knowledge on how to survive in life when you are gone. I remember I told you I got robbed and you told me that they should've stolen my damn Jordan shoes off my feet. I WILL FOREVER LOVE YOU!

Willie

ABOUT THE AUTHOR

Michael Stary, MD, is a career-long ER physician in South Florida. Willie Bentley is an African American male from the inner city in Miami. Collette Combs is a career educator in the Miami-Dade County School District.